Perfectly Portable

Picnic Recipes

Salads, Slaws, Sandwiches, Wraps, Savory
Snacks, and Sweet Treats to Go!

BY

Christina Tosch

Copyright Notes

vvvvvvvvvvvvvvvvvvvvvvvvvvvvvvvvvvvvvvvvvvvvvvvvvv

A special thank you for purchasing my book!

My sincerest thanks for purchasing my book! As added thanks, you are now eligible to receive a complimentary book sent to your email every week. To get started on this exclusive offer, fill in the box below by entering your email address and start receiving notifications of special promotions. It's not every day you get something for free for doing so little! Free and discounted books are available every day and a reminder will be sent to you so you never have to miss out. Fill in the box below and get started on this amazing offer!

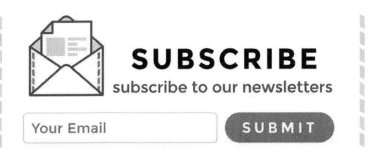

https://christina.subscribemenow.com

Table of Contents

Introduction

taking quality time out with family and friends is extremely important.

And what better way is there to sit back and relax, than taking to the great outdoors, laying a blanket on the ground and sharing a selection of perfect picnic foods?

Picnics however, are nothing new. In fact, the French first introduced them to the public in the late 18th century.

Fast forward to the 19th century which saw the launch of London's Picnic Society. Here, fashionable Londoners got together to share refreshments and entertainments.

It isn't just Europe who loves to picnic though!

Each year the White House in America's capital hosts their Congressional Picnic. This event is where members of Congress and their families get to spend time with the President and White House staff and enjoy picnic foods, music and carnival rides.

In 2019, while the Trumps tucked into an outdoor feast of fancy foods including grilled plank salmon, Baja shrimp tacos and locally grown fruit and veggies we bring you a collection of 40 perfectly-portable picnic recipes.

Discover easy-to-prepare picnic recipes, which include salads, slaws, sandwiches, wraps, savory snacks, and sweet treats.

Salads Slaws

Balsamic Three-Bean Salad

This three-bean salad is healthy, tasty, colorful, and picnic perfect.

Servings: 12

Total Time: 4hours 15mins

Ingredients:

- 2 pounds fresh green beans (trimmed, cut into 2" pieces)
- ½ cup balsamic vinaigrette
- ¼ cup sugar
- 1 garlic clove (peeled, minced)
- ¾ tsp salt
- 2 (16 ounce) cans kidney beans (rinsed, drained)
- 2 (15 ounce) cans cannellini beans (rinsed, drained)
- 4 fresh basil leaves (torn)

Directions:

1. Fill a Dutch oven ¾ full with water and bring to boil.

2. Add the green beans and uncovered, cook for between 3-6 minutes, until crisp yet tender. Drain and immediately plunge the beans into ice water. Drain the beans and using kitchen paper towel, pat dry.

3. In a bowl, whisk the balsamic vinaigrette with the sugar, garlic, and salt until the sugar is entirely dissolved.

4. Add the green beans, kidney beans, and cannellini beans to a bowl. Pour over the dressing and toss to coat evenly.

5. Cover and place in the fridge for a minimum of 4 hours.

6. When you are ready to serve, stir in the basil.

Broccoli Slaw with Lemon Dressing

Prepare this easy recipe at home, store it in your cooler bag, and take to the road.

Servings: 10

Total Time: 5mins

Ingredients:

- ½ cup sour cream
- 3 tbsp freshly squeezed lemon juice
- 2 tbsp full-fat mayonnaise
- 1 tbsp white wine vinegar
- 2 tsp lemon zest (grated)
- 1 tsp Dijon mustard
- ½ tsp salt
- ¼ tsp black pepper
- 1 (12 ounces) package broccoli coleslaw mix
- 2 large red apples (cored, julienned)

Directions:

1. In a bowl, combine the sour cream with the lemon juice, mayonnaise, vinegar, lemon zest, mustard, salt, and black pepper.

2. Add the broccoli coleslaw mix and apples and toss to coat evenly.

3. Cover and transfer to the fridge.

Couscous Salad

This couscous salad makes a great picnic filler.

Servings: 6-8

Total Time: 3hours 15mins

Ingredients:

- 1½ cups cooked couscous
- ½ cup extra-virgin olive oil
- 2 tbsp red onion (peeled, finely chopped)
- 2 tbsp freshly squeezed lemon juice
- 1-pint cherry tomatoes (halved)
- 2 tbsp fresh flat-leaf parsley (chopped)
- 1 English cucumber (unpeeled, seeded, finely chopped)
- 2 tbsp fresh mint (chopped)
- Sea salt and black pepper

Directions:

1. Prepare the couscous according to the package instructions. Using a fine-mesh strainer, drain and immediately rinse in cold running water. Drain again.

2. In a bowl, combine a ½ cup of olive oil with the onion, 2 tbsp of lemon juice, and whisk to incorporate.

3. Stir in the cooked couscous followed by the tomatoes, parsley, cucumber, and mint. Add a pinch of salt and a dash of pepper, to taste. Toss to combine evenly.

4. Cover and transfer to the fridge.

5. When you are ready to serve, remove from the fridge, and garnish with chopped parsley, fresh mint, and seasoning.

Curry Rice Salad

Rice salad gets an Indian-style makeover with curry powder, sultanas and peanuts.

Servings: 6

Total Time: 30mins

Ingredients:

- 1 cup long-grain white rice
- 1 tbsp curry powder
- 1 cup frozen corn with peas
- 1 green onion (sliced)
- 1 small-size carrot (grated)
- 1 small-size red capsicum (diced)
- 1 Lebanese cucumber (diced)
- 1 green apple (cored, diced)
- ⅓ cup sultanas
- 1 cup roasted salted peanuts (coarsely chopped)
- Green onion (sliced, to serve, optional)

Dressing:

- ⅓ cup store-bought French dressing
- 1 tsp curry powder
- 1 tbsp freshly squeezed lemon juice
- 1 tbsp brown sugar

Directions:

1. In a pan of boiling water, combine the rice with the curry powder, and cook at a boil, according to the package directions, until bite tender. Rinse the cooked rice under cold running water. Drain and put to one side to cool for 10-12 minutes.

2. In the meantime, cook the corn and peas, according to the package directions, until bite tender. Rinse under cold running water, drain and set aside to cool.

3. When cool, add the rice, corn, and peas to a mixing bowl. Stir in the onion followed by the carrot, capsicum, cucumber, apple, sultanas and roasted peanuts — season to taste.

4. For the dressing: Add the French dressing, curry powder, fresh lemon juice, and sugar to a jug, and stir to combine entirely.

5. Drizzle the dressing over the rice salad, toss to evenly coat and garnish with sliced green onion.

6. Pack in a suitable container and store in the fridge until ready to use.

Mayo-Free Potato Salad with Chives

Just because you aren't a fan of mayonnaise doesn't mean you can't enjoy a picnic-perfect potato salad.

Servings: 6

Total Time: 25mins

Ingredients:

- 2 pounds new potatoes
- ½ cup fresh chives (chopped)
- ⅓ cup olive oil
- 2 tbsp white wine vinegar
- 1 tsp Dijon mustard
- Sea salt
- Freshly ground black pepper
- 2 tbsp fresh-flat leaf parsley (chopped)

Directions:

1. In a pan of salted water, simmer the potatoes until fork tender. Rinse under cold running water, to cool before slicing into quarters.

2. Place the potatoes in a mixing bowl.

3. In a blender puree the chives along with the oil, vinegar, and mustard. Season with salt and pepper.

4. Pour the mixture over the potatoes, add the parsley and toss to combine evenly.

5. Transfer to the fridge until you are ready to serve.

Pear, Walnut, and Feta Salad

A marriage made in culinary heaven, fruit, nuts, and cheese
– you will love this picnic salad.

Servings: 4

Total Time: 6mins

Ingredients:

- 4 cups Romaine lettuce (chopped)
- 2 ripe pears (cored, cut into spears)
- ½ cup dried cranberries
- ½ cup walnuts (chopped)
- ½ cup Feta cheese (crumbled)
- Balsamic vinegar (to serve)

Directions:

1. Add the lettuce followed by the pears, cranberries, walnuts, and feta cheese to a mixing bowl and toss to combine evenly.

2. Transfer to the fridge, to chill.

3. When you are ready to serve drizzle with balsamic vinegar.

Ruby Raspberry Slaw

This crunchy, colorful slaw is berrylicious!

Servings: 6

Total Time: 15mins

Ingredients:

- 2 cups white cabbage (shredded)
- 2 cups red cabbage (shredded)
- 1 cup carrots (shredded)
- ¼ cup store-bought raspberry vinaigrette
- 3 tbsp mayonnaise
- ¼ tsp freshly ground black pepper
- ½ cup fresh raspberries

Directions:

1. In a bowl, combine the white and red cabbage with the shredded carrots.

2. In a smaller bowl, whisk the raspberry vinaigrette with the mayonnaise and black pepper until combined.

3. Add the vinaigrette to the cabbage mixture and toss to coat evenly.

4. Place in the fridge, covered, for 10-15 minutes to chill.

5. When you are ready to pack your picnic, remove from the fridge, and top with fresh raspberries.

6. Enjoy.

Summer Slaw with Chilli Mango Mayo

Enjoy a real taste of summer with this healthy homemade slaw.

Servings: 4

Total Time: 20mins

Ingredients:

Dressing:

- 1 mango (peeled, pitted, diced)
- ¼ cup sweet chilli sauce
- 2 tbsp full-fat mayonnaise

Slaw:

- ½ Chinese cabbage (shredded)
- 1¾ ounces baby spinach (shredded)
- 1¾ ounces rocket leaves (shredded)
- 1 corncob (cooked, cooled)
- ½ red capsicum (thinly sliced)
- 2 mangos (peeled, pitted, thinly sliced)
- ¼ cup coconut flakes
- 2 shallots (thinly sliced)

Directions:

1. In a food blender, combine the mango with the sweet chili sauce and mayonnaise, and on high, process until silky smooth. Transfer to the fridge to chill.

2. Layer the first 6 salad ingredients in recipe order (Chinese cabbage, baby spinach, rocket leaves, corncob, red capsicum, and mango).

3. Top with coconut flakes and shallots.

4. Transfer to the fridge until ready to serve.

5. Fold the mango mayo into the slaw just before serving.

Three-Pasta Salad in a Jar

Catering for a crowd? Then this picnic party pleasing salad in a jar will tick all the boxes.

Servings: 16

Total Time: 15mins

Ingredients:

- 8 ounces uncooked farfalle pasta
- 8 ounces uncooked rotelle pasta
- 8 ounces uncooked pasta shells
- 2 cups Greek-style vinaigrette
- 3 cups cherry tomatoes (halved)
- 1 medium red onion (peeled, finely chopped)
- 1 (12 ounce) jar marinated quartered artichoke hearts (drained, coarsely chopped)
- 1 (12 ounce) jar roasted sweet red peppers (drained, chopped)
- 1 cup fresh basil (chopped)
- 1 cup Parmesan cheese (freshly grated)
- 1 (3½ ounce) package sliced pepperoni
- 1(2¼ ounce) can sliced ripe olives (drained)

Directions:

1. In boiling salted water, cook the various pasta until al dente. Drain and rinse under cold running water. Drain once again before transferring to a mixing bowl.

2. Add the vinaigrette to the drained pasta and toss to coat evenly.

3. Next, add the cherry tomatoes, red onion, artichoke hearts and red peppers followed by the basil, Parmesan cheese, pepperoni, and olives. Toss well to combine evenly.

4. Transfer to Mason jars, and place in the fridge until ready to enjoy.

Watermelon, Cherry Tomato, and Feta Salad

This refreshing salad is family-friendly, super colorful, and just what you need to re-hydrate in the hot sunshine.

Servings: 6

Total Time: 4mins

Ingredients:

- 1 (3 pound) watermelon (rind removed, seeded, cut into 1½" thick triangles)
- ½ cup fresh mint
- ¼ cup red onion (peeled, thinly sliced)
- 12 ounces cherry tomatoes (halved)
- 2 tbsp olive oil
- 2 tbsp fresh lime juice
- 1 tsp runny honey
- Sea salt and freshly ground black pepper
- Feta cheese (crumbled)

Directions:

1. Arrange the watermelon on a platter.

2. Top with mint, onion and cherry tomatoes.

3. In a bowl, combine the oil with the lime juice, honey, sea salt, and black pepper, mix to incorporate.

4. Pour the dressing over the watermelon and scatter with crumbled feta cheese.

Sandwiches Wraps

BLT and Chipotle Mayo Wraps

Who doesn't like a BLT, and you will love these wraps served with a spicy, tangy chipotle mayonnaise.

Servings: 4

Total Time: 6mins

Ingredients:

- 3 cups romaine lettuce (chopped)
- 2 plum tomatoes (finely chopped)
- 8 bacon strips (cooked, crumbled)
- ⅓ cup chipotle mayonnaise
- 4 (8") flour tortillas (warmed)

Directions:

1. In a bowl, combine the romaine lettuce, tomatoes, and bacon. Stir in the mayonnaise; tossing to coat.

2. Spoon approximately 1 cup of the romaine mixture down the middle of each tortilla. Fold the bottom of the tortilla over to cover the filling; fold both sides to close.

3. Transfer to a suitable container and serve when needed.

Chicken, Pistachio and Mayo Sandwiches

Crunchy pistachio nuts give great texture to this chicken mayo sandwich filler.

Servings: 6

Total Time: 45mins

Ingredients:

- 3 skin-on, chicken breasts skin off
- Pinch of salt
- Dash of pepper
- Spring of fresh rosemary
- 1 cup mayonnaise
- 2 tbsp sour cream
- 3 tbsp pistachios (chopped)
- 2 tbsp chives (chopped)
- 6 tsp butter (room temperature)
- 12 slices bread (crusts removed)

Directions:

1. In a pan, heat sufficient water to cover the chicken breasts.

2. Add a pinch of salt, a dash of pepper and the rosemary sprigs. Once the water begins to bubble, add the chicken.

3. Cover the pan, and over very low heat, simmer for between 5-6 minutes. Set aside for 10 minutes, to allow the chicken to cool before removing it and draining. Set the chicken to one side for several minutes, before shredding.

4. Add the shredded chicken along with the mayonnaise, sour cream, pistachios, and chives to a mixing bowl, and mix to combine.

5. Butter the bread on both sides, top 6 slices of bread with the chicken mixture. Place the remaining slices on top to form sandwiches and enjoy.

Crab Rolls to Go

Lose the lobster and instead opt for these creamy crab rolls with crisp lettuce. They are picnic perfect.

Servings: 2

Total Time: 5mins

Ingredients:

- 8 ounces fresh crabmeat (chilled)
- 2 tbsp mayonnaise (chilled)
- Sea salt
- 2 tbsp unsalted butter (room temperature)
- 2 hot dog buns (split)
- Lettuce leaves (torn, to serve)
- Freshly ground white pepper (to season)

Directions:

1. In a bowl, gently mix the fresh crab with the mayonnaise until combined. Season with salt

2. Over moderate heat, heat a large frying pan.

3. Butter the flat sides of each bun and fry in the pan for a couple of minutes on each side, until golden.

4. Fill each bun with the torn lettuce, and crab mayo.

5. Season to taste with white pepper.

6. Enjoy.

Crispy Coconut Shrimp Sandwich

Heading out to the Keys or enjoying a picnic on your front porch? Regardless of whether you are home or away, you will love this crispy coconut shrimp sandwich.

Servings: 4

Total Time: 25mins

Ingredients:

- ½ cup panko breadcrumbs
- ½ cup shredded coconut
- Kosher salt
- Freshly ground black pepper
- 1 large-size egg
- 3 tbsp cornstarch
- 20 jumbo shrimp (peeled, deveined)
- 4 tbsp olive oil
- 4 hoagie rolls
- Mayonnaise
- Sriracha sauce
- Cucumber (sliced)
- Radishes
- Jalapeno (sliced)
- Scallions (sliced)
- Cilantro (chopped)
- Lime wedges (to serve)

Directions:

1. In a bowl, combine the panko breadcrumbs with the shredded coconut along with ¼ tsp each of salt and pepper.

2. In a shallow bowl, beat the egg.

3. Add the cornstarch to a second shallow bowl,

4. One shrimp at a time, dip the shrimp first in the cornstarch, then the eggs, and lastly in the coconut mixture. Gently press the mixture into the shrimp.

5. Over moderate heat, heat 2 tbsp of oil in a large frying pan.

6. Add half the shrimp to the pan, and cook until opaque and golden, for 1-2 minutes on each side. Transfer the golden shrimp to a plate.

7. Wipe the pan with kitchen paper towel and repeat the process with the remaining 2 tbsp of oil and shrimp.

8. Evenly spread the rolls with the mayonnaise and Sriracha sauce.

9. Evenly divide the shrimp between the rolls and top with the slices of cucumber, radishes, jalapeno, cilantro, and scallions.

10. Serve with wedges of lime.

Curried Egg and Lettuce Sandwiches

You will never again be a few sandwiches short of a picnic when you make a batch of these scrumptious sandwiches.

Servings: 4-8

Total Time: 5mins

Ingredients:

- 4 eggs hard-boiled (peeled)
- ½ tsp curry powder
- 1⅓ tbsp milk
- 1 tbsp butter
- 1 Iceberg lettuce (cored, cleaned, shredded)
- 8 slices of brown seeded bread

Directions:

1. Add the eggs to a bowl along with the curry powder, milk, and butter, and mash to combine.

2. Place the lettuce on 4 slices of seeded bread, top with the curried egg mixture.

3. Place the remaining slices of seeded bread on top, to form 4 sandwiches. Cut into triangles and serve.

Greek-Style Chickpea Gyros

You may not be enjoying your picnic while watching the sunset over the Aegean, but that doesn't mean you can't enjoy a Greek-style snack, and this veggie gyros is simply delicious wherever you are!

Servings: 4

Total Time: 35mins

Ingredients:

- 1 (14 ½ ounce) can chickpeas (drained, rinsed, patted dry)
- 1 tbsp extra-virgin olive oil
- 1 tbsp paprika
- 1 tsp freshly ground black pepper
- ½ tsp cayenne pepper
- ¼ tsp salt
- 4 pita flatbreads
- 1 cup store-bought tzatziki
- ¼ red onion (peeled, cut into strips)
- 2 lettuce leaves (coarsely torn)
- 1 tomato (sliced)

Directions:

1. Preheat the main oven to 400 degrees F.

2. Remove any chickpeas skins that have come loose.

3. In a bowl, toss the chickpeas with the olive oil, paprika, black pepper, cayenne pepper and salt.

4. Evenly spread the chickpeas on a lightly greased baking sheet and roast for approximately 20 minutes, until gently browned but not hard.

5. To assemble: Spoon the tzatziki on one side of the flatbreads. Sprinkle in a quarter of the chickpeas and add the onion, lettuce, and tomato.

6. Fold the flatbreads in half and serve.

Greek-Style Sausage Wraps

These tasty sausage wraps are sure to be a highlight of your next picnic.

Servings: 4

Total Time: 30mins

Ingredients:

- 7 ounces store-bought tzatziki
- 4 flatbreads
- 2 cups lettuce (chopped)
- 4 fresh tomatoes (sliced)
- 2 red onions (peeled, sliced)
- 8 cooked, lamb, pork or beef sausages

Directions:

1. Spread the tzatziki evenly over the flatbreads.

2. Top with lettuce, sliced tomato, and onions.

3. Lay 2 sausages on top and firmly roll.

4. Serve and enjoy.

Ham and Minted Pea Sandwiches

Impromptu picnic never fear you can whip up a quick deli-style sandwich in a matter of minutes, and you are good to go!

Servings: 2

Total Time: 3mins

Ingredients:

- 1 cup frozen minted peas (defrosted)
- 2 tbsp Dijon mustard
- ¼ cup mayonnaise
- 4 slices roast deli ham
- 4 slices of brown bread

Directions:

1. Add the peas to a food blender, and pulse until lightly chopped.

2. In a bowl, combine the mustard and mayonnaise.

3. Butter one side of each slice of bread with the mustard mayo and top with ham.

4. Spoon the peas on top of the ham.

5. Place the remaining two slices of bread on top to form two sandwiches.

Mexican Wraps

Turn your picnic into a fiesta with these protein-packed Mexican wraps.

Servings: 6

Total Time: 30mins

Ingredients:

- 1 pound minced beef
- 10½ ounces salsa
- 1 (14 ounce) can red kidney beans (drained, rinsed)
- 6 flatbreads or mountain bread wraps
- 4 cups reduced-fat Cheddar cheese (grated)
- 5½ ounces low-fat sour cream

Directions:

1. In a bowl, combine the minced beef with the salsa and kidney beans.

2. Spread between 3-4 tbsp of the beef-bean mixture down the middle of each wrap.

3. Sprinkle with the grated cheese.

4. Fold the edges over to enclose the filling.

5. In a pan, over moderate to high heat, toast the flatbread on one side only.

6. Remove the wrap from the pan and place on a plate.

7. Open the wrap, add the sour cream.

8. Close, return to the pan and toast on the other side.

9. Remove from the pan and set aside to cool.

10. You can enjoy these wraps warm or cold.

Pastrami Pickle Roll-Ups

Salty pastrami combines with sharp dill pickles and delicious creamy cheese for a savory snack.

Servings: 4

Total Time: 10mins

Ingredients:

- 4 small tortillas
- 8 slices of pastrami
- 4 ounces cream cheese
- Pinch of paprika
- 2 tsp dill (chopped)
- 4 medium-size dill pickles
- Freshly ground black pepper

Directions:

1. Spread a thin and even layer of cream cheese on each tortilla.

2. Sprinkle paprika and dill over the cheese.

3. Arrange 2 slices of pastrami on top of each tortilla.

4. Place a dill pickle in the middle of the pastrami.

5. Season with black pepper.

6. Gently but tightly roll the tortilla up before slicing into 1" chunks and serving. You may need to secure the chunks using cocktails sticks.

Savory Snacks

Cola Chicken Wings

Chicken wings have to be top of any picnic party menu, and these cola wings sure are tasty!

Servings: 4

Total Time: 1hour

Ingredients:

- 16 chicken wings (washed, dried, patted dry)
- ½ tsp salt
- ½ cup cola
- ¼ cup brown sugar
- 1 tbsp tomato paste
- 1 clove garlic, (peeled, minced)
- ½ tsp dried red chilli flakes
- 1 tsp paprika
- 1 whole green onion (finely sliced, to garnish)

Directions:

1. Preheat the main oven to 450 degrees F. Using parchment paper line a baking sheet. Set the sheet to one side.

2. Arrange the wings in a single layer on the baking sheet, allowing at least 1" of space between each one. Scatter half of the salt over the wings.

3. Bake in the preheated oven for 20 minutes.

4. Remove the wings from the oven and flip over, season with the remaining salt and bake in the oven for an additional 20 minutes.

5. Meanwhile, add the cola, brown sugar, tomato paste, garlic, red chili flakes and paprika to a frying pan.

6. Over moderate to high heat, whisk the ingredients and allow to come to a low boil while the sauce thickens.

7. Remove the wings from the oven and add to the frying pan.

8. Toss to evenly coat, and over moderate-high heat cook until the wings have absorbed all of the sauce and the wings are beginning to char.

9. Take the wings out of the frying pan and transfer to a platter.

10. Set aside to cool before storing in a suitable container until you are ready to prepare your picnic.

Corned Beef and Swiss Mini Pot Pies

All the flavors of a Reuben sandwich but in the form of a mini pot pie. Who can resist?

Servings: 8

Total Time: 40mins

Ingredients:

- Nonstick baking spray
- 8 ounces corned beef (thinly sliced, coarsely chopped)
- 1 cup Swiss cheese (shredded)
- 1 (10¾ ounce) can condensed low-salt cream of mushroom soup
- 1 tbsp Dijon mustard
- 1 tsp caraway seeds
- 1 (16⅓ ounce) can flaky layered refrigerated biscuits

Directions:

1. Preheat the main oven to 375 degrees F.

2. Lightly spritz an 8-cup standard muffin pan with nonstick baking spray.

3. In a bowl, combine the corned beef with the Swiss cheese, condensed soup, Dijon mustard, and caraway seeds.

4. Separate the dough into 8 biscuits.

5. Gently press each biscuit into a 5½" round.

6. Spoon 1/3 cup of the corned beef mixture into the middle of each pastry round.

7. Pull the edges of the pastry up gently to enclose the filling and place into the muffin cups.

8. Pull the edges of the dough over to cover the filling towards the middle, pleat and gently pinch the dough to hold it in place, leaving some of the filling exposed.

9. Bake in the preheated oven for 20-25 minutes, until golden.

10. Set aside to cool for 60 seconds, before removing from the pan.

11. Allow to completely cool before transferring to a suitable picnic food container.

12. Enjoy.

Falafel Balls

These tasty mini quiches are packed with ham, olive, and cheddar cheese and flavored with pepper sauce and mustard for a small snack with big flavor.

Servings: 12

Total Time: 8hours 40mins

Ingredients:

- 2½ cups dried chickpeas
- 1 tsp canola oil
- 2 yellow onions (peeled, finely diced)
- 4 cloves garlic (peeled, minced)
- 1 tsp cumin seeds
- Small bunch fresh parsley
- ¼ tsp cayenne pepper
- 2 tsp fresh lemon juice
- Black pepper
- ½ tsp baking powder
- 2 tsp salt
- ⅔ cup chickpea flour
- 3 tbsp olive oil

Directions:

1. Add the chickpeas to a large bowl and cover with water. Cover and allow to soak overnight until doubled in size.

2. The following day, warm the canola oil in a pan over moderately high heat. Add the onion, garlic, and cumin seeds. Sauté for 5 minutes until browned.

3. Drain the chickpeas and rinse clean.

4. Preheat the main oven to 400 degrees F.

5. In batches, add the chickpeas to a food processor and pulse until finely chopped.

6. Next, add the parsley to the processor to chop fine.

7. Combine the chickpeas and parsley to a large bowl along with the cayenne pepper, lemon juice, black pepper, baking powder, and salt. Mix until well combined.

8. Next, mix in the chickpea flour and olive oil.

9. Roll the mixture into 2" balls and arrange on a baking tray.

10. Place in the oven and bake for approximately 25 minutes until golden.

11. Serve warm or cooled.

Garlic and Herb Pint-Size Pizzas

Pint-size pizzas with flavorful garlic and Italian herbs will go down a treat with both youngsters and grownups.

Servings: 8

Total Time: 20mins

Ingredients:

- ½ cup mayonnaise
- 1⅓ cups mozzarella cheese (shredded)
- ½ tsp garlic powder
- 1½ tsp dried oregano
- ¼ tsp black pepper
- ¼ tsp salt
- 4 English muffins (halved)

Directions:

1. Preheat your oven's broiler and position a rack 3-4" from the heat.

2. In a bowl, stir together the mayonnaise, mozzarella cheese, garlic powder, oregano, black pepper, and salt.

3. Spread the mixture equally onto the muffin halves.

4. Arrange the mini pizzas on the rack and broil for several minutes until golden and bubbly.

5. Serve warm or cooled.

Mini Pork Pies with Caramelized Onion

A savory snack makes an ideal picnic treat, and these pies are sure to be a winner.

Servings: 12

Total Time: 25mins

Ingredients:

- 1 tbsp olive oil
- 1 red onion (peeled, thinly sliced)
- 1 white onion (peeled, thinly sliced)
- 1 tbsp soft brown sugar
- 1 (1 pound) package store-bought, ready-made puff pastry
- 4 chunky pork sausages (skinned)
- 1 medium-size egg
- Splash of milk (to glaze)

Directions:

1. Preheat the main oven to 350 degrees F.

2. In a small pan, heat the oil.

3. Add the red and white onions to the pan, and gently cook until softened, but not brown.

4. Next, add the brown sugar and mix to combine until the mixture is heated through and the onions are caramelized. Set aside to slightly cool.

5. Roll the pastry out, and line a 12-cup muffin or fairy cake pan with pastry.

6. In a bowl, combine the sausage meat with the onions. Add a small spoonful of the sausage meat mixture into each cup.

7. Cut out 12 pastry lids and brush a drop of water onto the edges of each one. Place the damp edge facing downwards onto the mixture, and gently press to seal the edges.

8. In a small bowl, combine the egg with the milk to make a glaze.

9. Using a knife, pierce a small hole in the top of the pie, to allow steam to escape and lightly brush with the egg-milk glaze.

10. Transfer to the oven and cook until golden and rises, for 15-20 minutes.

11. Remove from the oven and set aside to cool.

12. Pack your picnic and enjoy.

Miniature Ham Quiches

These tasty mini quiches are packed with ham, olive, and cheddar cheese and flavored with pepper sauce and mustard for a small snack with big flavor.

Servings: 12

Total Time: 35mins

Ingredients:

- Butter (to grease)
- ¾ cup cooked ham (diced)
- ½ cup olives (stoned, chopped)
- ½ cup cheddar cheese (shredded)
- 3 eggs (beaten lightly)
- ¼ cup melted butter
- 1 cup half half
- ½ cup baking mix
- 3 dashes hot pepper sauce
- 2 tbsp parmesan cheese (grated)
- ½ tsp mustard powder

Directions:

1. Preheat the main oven to 375 degrees F. Grease 12 muffin cups.

2. In a bowl, combine the ham, olives, and cheddar. Divide between the muffin cups.

3. In a second bowl, stir together the eggs, melted butter, half half, baking mix, hot pepper sauce, parmesan cheese, and mustard powder until combined. Pour the mixture evenly into the muffin cups.

4. Place in the oven and bake for just over 20 minutes until golden and set in the center.

5. Serve warm or cooled.

Picnic Eggs

A tasty twist on the British picnic classic; Scotch eggs!

Servings: 4

Total Time: 35mins

Ingredients:

- 10 hard-boiled eggs (peeled)
- 8¾ ounces sliced cooked ham (diced)
- 2 tbsp Cheddar cheese (grated)
- 2 yellow onions (peeled, diced)
- 7 green chillies (seeded, diced)
- Salt and black pepper
- 2 eggs (beaten)
- Semolina (for coating)
- Olive oil

Directions:

1. Slice the hard-boiled eggs lengthwise in half and carefully scoop out the yolk. Add the yolk and the whites to separate bowls.

2. Mash the cooked egg yolk then stir in the ham, Cheddar cheese, onion, and chilies. When combined and malleable, season to taste with salt and black pepper.

3. Roll the yolk mixture into 4 balls and place each ball in the well of 4 of the reserved egg white halves.

4. Top each filled egg white half with a second egg white half to create 4 whole eggs.

5. Dip each whole egg first in beaten egg and then in semolina.

6. Heat olive oil in a deep fryer. Deep fry the eggs until golden brown and crisp.

Prawn and Egg Vol-Au-Vents

Pop in the mouth juicy prawn and egg vol-au-vents are the quintessential picnic nibble.

Servings: 12

Total Time: 15mins

Ingredients:

- 1½ pounds cooked prawns (shelled, deveined)
- 6 hard-boiled eggs (peeled, chopped)
- 2 tbsp olives (pitted, chopped)
- 2 tbsp chives (chopped)
- 4 tbsp full-fat mayonnaise
- 12 large vol-au-vent cases
- Sprigs of dill (to garnish)

Directions:

1. First, chop half of the prawns while leaving the other half, tails-on.

2. In a mixing bowl, combine the chopped hard-boiled eggs with the chopped prawns, olives, and chives.

3. Gradually, a teaspoon at a time, stir in the mayonnaise, until a slightly stiff consistency.

4. Spoon the egg and mayonnaise mixture into the 12 vol-au-vent cases.

5. Top with the whole prawns and garnish with sprigs of dill.

Prosciutto and Sage Pinwheels

Buttery golden pastry pinwheels filled with aromatic sage, salty prosciutto, and tangy honey mustard are simply irresistible. Be sure to bake plenty; they'll go quick!

Servings: 36

Total Time: 35mins

Ingredients:

- Butter (to grease)
- 1 (17.3 ounce) package frozen puff pastry (thawed)
- ¼ cup honey mustard
- 1 cup Swiss cheese (shredded)
- 2 tbsp fresh sage (chopped)
- 8 slices prosciutto (chopped)

Directions:

1. Preheat the main oven to 400 degrees F. Grease 2 baking sheets.

2. Unfold one of the pastry sheets. Spread 2 tbsp of honey mustard over the pastry sheet, leaving a ½" border-free. Sprinkle over half of the cheese, sage, and prosciutto.

3. Roll up the pastry sheet as you would a jelly roll. Using a serrated knife, slice the roll widthwise to create 18 pinwheels.

4. Repeat with the second pastry sheet and remaining ingredients.

5. Arrange the pinwheels on the baking sheets.

6. Place in the oven and bake for 12-15 minutes until golden.

7. Serve warm or cooled.

Veggie Tofu Kebabs

A delicious vegan option for your picnic spread.

Servings: 6

Total Time: 35mins

Ingredients:

- 1 (6.3 ounce) block tofu (pressed to extract liquid, cubed)
- 2 tbsp soy sauce
- 2 small zucchinis (sliced)
- 1 red onion (peeled, cut into squares
- 2 bell peppers (cut into squares)
- 2 cups cherry tomatoes
- Olive oil
- Salt and black pepper
- 3 tsp BBQ sauce
- 2 tsp sesame seeds
- Bamboo skewers

Directions:

1. Add the tofu and soy sauce to a bowl and set aside to marinate.

2. Thread the tofu cubes and veggies alternately onto bamboo skewers.

3. Preheat a grill to high heat and grease with olive oil.

4. Place the skewers on the grill and cook until the tofu begins to turn golden and the vegetables soften.

5. Season the skewers with salt and black pepper, then brush with BBQ sauce. Sprinkle over the sesame seeds. Grill for 60 seconds more before taking off the heat.

6. Serve hot or cooled.

Sweet Treats

Cherry Choc Chunk Cookies

Not just any cookies, these decadent delights are studded with melting chocolate chunks and chewy cherries. This sweet treat is the perfect addition to any picnic blanket.

Servings: 48

Total Time: 45mins

Ingredients:

- 1 cup cocoa powder
- 1½ cups all-purpose flour
- 1 tsp salt
- 1 tsp bicarb of soda
- 1¼ cups dark brown sugar
- ¾ cup granulated sugar
- 1 cup unsalted butter
- 2 large eggs
- 2 tsp vanilla essence
- 1½ cups dried chart cherries
- 1½ cups bittersweet chocolate (chopped)

Directions:

1. Preheat the main oven to 350 degrees F. Line 2 baking pans with parchment and set to one side.

2. In a bowl, combine the cocoa powder, flour, salt, and bicarb of soda. Set to one side.

3. Next, beat together the brown sugar, granulated sugar, and butter using an electric mixer until fluffy.

4. Beat in the eggs one at a time followed by the vanilla essence.

5. With the electric mixer on low speed, mix in the flour a little at a time.

6. Fold in the cherries and chopped chocolate.

7. Taking 2 tbsp of dough at a time, roll the cookie dough into balls and place on the baking sheets. Ensure the dough balls do not touch.

8. Place in the oven and bake for approximately 12 minutes. Allow the cookies to cool completely before serving.

Honeycomb and Peanut Rocky Road

Melt in the mouth honeycomb candy is a fun and tasty addition to classic rocky road.

Servings: 24

Total Time: 8hours 15mins

Ingredients:

- 7 ounces milk chocolate
- 7 ounces dark chocolate
- 1 tbsp golden syrup
- 2½ tbsp salted butter
- 3½ ounces mini marshmallows
- 3½ ounces salted peanuts
- 2½ chocolate covered honeycomb candy bars (chopped)

Directions:

1. Line an 8-9" square tin with a double layer of plastic wrap.

2. Using a double boiler, melt together the milk chocolate, dark chocolate, golden syrup, and salted butter until silky and combined.

3. Fold in the marshmallows, peanuts, and a chopped candy bar.

4. Take off the heat and pour into the prepared pan. Smooth out the surface using a rubber spatula.

5. Chill overnight until set before slicing into bars/squares and serving.

Key Lime Fudge

Bite into your favorite summer Floridian dessert in picnic-friendly fudge form.

Servings: 16-18

Total Time: 8hours 15mins

Ingredients:

- 5 ounces evaporated milk
- 1⅔ cup granulated sugar
- ½ tsp kosher salt
- 12 extra-large marshmallows (sliced in half)
- 2 cups white chocolate chips
- Zest and juice of 5 Key limes

Directions:

1. Line a square baking tin with parchment.

2. In a saucepan, bring to a boil the evaporated milk, granulated sugar, and kosher salt. Allow to boil for several minutes, stirring continuously.

3. Take off the heat and add the marshmallows, white chocolate chips, Key lime zest, and juice. Stir well until all ingredients are combined.

4. Transfer the mix into the baking tin and refrigerate overnight until set before slicing into squares and enjoying.

Lemon Cream Sandwich Cookies

Disguise store-bought cookies with a velvety smooth homemade lemon cream for a sweet snack that is both delicious and low maintenance!

Servings: 16

Total Time: 15mins

Ingredients:

- 2 ounces full-fat cream cheese (at room temperature)
- 3 tbsp confectioner's sugar
- 2 tbsp fresh lemon juice
- ½ tsp fresh lemon zest
- ½ cup heavy cream
- 32 thin lemon cookies

Directions:

1. Using an electric mixer, beat the cream cheese until fluffy.

2. Add the confectioner's sugar, lemon juice, and zest, and beat again to combine.

3. With the mixer running, add the heavy cream a splash at a time until the mixture can hold stiff peaks.

4. Spread approximately 2 teaspoons of lemon cream onto 16 of the lemon cookies. Sandwich together with the remaining cookies.

5. Store in an airtight container.

Macadamia and White Choc Chunk Blondies

White chocolate and macadamia nuts are a match made in heaven, especially when concealed in gooey blondie batter.

Servings: 25

Total Time: 30mins

Ingredients:

- ½ cup melted unsalted butter
- 1 cup light brown sugar
- 1 egg
- 1 tsp vanilla essence
- Pinch kosher salt
- 1 cup all-purpose flour
- ½ cup macadamia nuts
- ½ cup white chocolate chunks

Directions:

1. Preheat the main oven to 350 degrees F. Line an 8" square dish with parchment and set to one side.

2. Beat together the butter and light brown sugar. Next, beat in the egg and vanilla until combined.

3. Fold in the kosher salt, and all-purpose flour until well incorporated.

4. Next, fold in macadamia nuts and white chocolate chunks.

5. Transfer the mixture to the prepared dish and place in the oven for just over 20 minutes until golden.

6. Take out of the oven and allow to cool before slicing into squares and serving.

7. Store in an airtight container at room temperature.

Peach, Strawberry, and Basil Bars

These fruity treats with aromatic fresh basil offer a taste of summer with every bite.

Servings: 24

Total Time: 1hour 15mins

Ingredients:

- Butter (to grease)

Base:

- 3 cups flour
- 1 cup granulated sugar
- 1 tsp baking powder
- ¼ tsp cinnamon
- ¼ tsp salt
- 1 cup salted butter (chilled)
- 1 medium egg

Filling:

- 3 cups fresh peach (peeled and diced)
- 2 cups fresh strawberries (hulled, diced)
- ¼ cup fresh basil leaves (chiffonaded)
- Juice of 1 medium lemon
- ½ cup granulated sugar
- ½ cup flour
- ¼ tsp cardamom
- ½ tsp cinnamon
- ¼ tsp salt

Directions:

1. Preheat the main oven to 375 degrees F. Grease a 13x9" baking tin with butter.

2. First, prepare the crust. Combine the flour, sugar, and baking powder in a bowl. Stir in the cinnamon and salt.

3. Add the butter and egg to the dry ingredients and cut in using two knives. The dough should be crumbly.

4. Pat half of the dough mixture into the prepared baking tin in an even layer.

5. Next, prepare the filling. Toss the peach, strawberry, basil, and lemon juice together in a bowl then set to one side.

6. In a second small bowl, combine the sugar, flour, cardamom, cinnamon, and salt. Scatter the mixture over the fruit and gently toss to combine.

7. Arrange the fruit mixture on top of the crust then top with the remaining crust.

8. Place in the oven and bake for approximately 45 minutes until golden brown.

9. Allow to cool completely before slicing into squares.

Pina Colada Balls

With all the flavor of the classic cocktail without the booze, these tropical-tasting balls are perfect for the kids and the grownups!

Servings: 24

Total Time: 8hours 20mins

Ingredients:

- 1 (8 ounce) can crushed pineapple (juice drained away)
- 8 ounces full-fat cream cheese
- 2½ cups shredded sweetened coconut

Directions:

1. Beat together the pineapple and cream cheese in a small bowl until fluffy and combined.

2. Cover the bowl with plastic wrap and chill for half an hour.

3. Roll the mixture into 1" balls and then roll each ball in shredded coconut until evenly coated.

4. Chill overnight until firm.

Pretty in Pink Popcorn Balls

Your little ones will go crazy for these sticky-sweet popcorn balls thanks to their marshmallow-like texture and pretty pink color.

Servings: 24

Total Time: 20mins

Ingredients:

- ¼ cup margarine
- ¾ cup light corn syrup
- 2 tsp water (cold)
- 2½ cups confectioner's sugar
- 1 cup marshmallows
- Few drops pink/red food coloring
- 20 cups popped plain popcorn

Directions:

1. In a saucepan over moderate heat, combine the margarine, corn syrup, cold water, confectioner's sugar, marshmallows, and pink food coloring.

2. Bring the mixture to a boil while stirring.

3. In the meantime, add the popcorn to a large bowl. Pour the marshmallow mixture over the popcorn and stir until evenly coated.

4. Allow the mixture to cool enough to handle.

5. Butter your fingers and roll the mixture into 3½" balls.

6. Wrap each ball with plastic wrap and store at room temperature.

Salted Caramel Cheesecake Bars

Finish your picnic with an indulgent piece of rich salted caramel cheesecake which sets firm, perfect for enjoying out of the house.

Servings: 9

Total Time: 1hour 45mins

Ingredients:

- Nonstick cooking spray

Base:

- 12 graham cracker sheets
- ¼ cup granulated sugar
- ½ cup melted butter
- Cheesecake Layer:
- ⅓ cup granulated sugar
- 1 egg (room temperature)
- 1 pound full-fat cream cheese (at room temperature)
- 2 tsp vanilla essence
- ⅓ cup salted caramel sauce

Directions:

1. Preheat the main oven to 350 degrees F. Line an 8" square baking tin with aluminum foil and spritz with nonstick cooking spray.

2. Add the graham crackers and sugar to a food processor and pulse until combined and a fine crumb.

3. Add the melted butter and pulse until the mixture comes together.

4. Press the graham cracker mixture into the base of the prepared tin.

5. Place in the oven and bake for 5 minutes.

6. In the meantime, beat together the sugar, egg, cream cheese, and vanilla essence until fluffy and combined.

7. Spread the mixture on top of the half baked base.

8. Drop teaspoons of salted caramel sauce on top of the cheesecake mixture and swirl using a knife. Place in the oven and bake for 20 minutes.

9. Allow to cool before transferring to the refrigerator to cool completely before slicing.

Spiced Pear Cakes

Soft and moist individual pear cakes spiced with nutmeg and cinnamon will perfectly complement a spread of colourful salads and tasty sandwiches.

Servings: 9

Total Time: 45mins

Ingredients:

- Butter and flour (for tart tins)
- ¾ tsp baking powder
- 1½ cups all-purpose flour
- ¼ tsp salt
- 1½ tsp bicarb of soda
- ¾ cup granulated sugar
- 6 tbsp unsalted butter
- ½ tsp ground cinnamon
- 1 tsp fresh grated nutmeg
- 1 large egg
- 1½ tsp vanilla essence
- ¼ cup + 2 tbsp sour cream
- 1 cup sweet pears (chopped)
- 9 slices of pear (for topping)

Directions:

1. Preheat the main oven to 400 degrees F.

2. Grease and flour nine 4" mini tart tins.

3. In a bowl, combine the baking powder, flour, salt, and bicarb of soda.

4. Using an electric mixer, beat together the sugar and butter until fluffy. Next, add the cinnamon, nutmeg, egg, and vanilla essence. Mix until combined.

5. With the mixer running on low speed, add the flour mixture a little at a time alternating with sour cream until both are incorporated.

6. Fold in the chopped pears.

7. Pour a ⅓ of a cup of cake batter into each tart tin and top each with a slice of pear for decoration.

8. Bake in the oven for 20 minutes. Allow to cool before serving.

Author's Afterthoughts

thank you

I would like to express my deepest thanks to you, the reader, for making this investment in one my books. I cherish the thought of bringing the love of cooking into your home.

With so much choice out there, I am grateful you decided to Purch this book and read it from beginning to end.

Please let me know by submitting an Amazon review if you enjoyed this book and found it contained valuable information to help you in your culinary endeavors. Please take a few minutes to express your opinion freely and honestly. This will help others make an informed decision on purchasing and provide me with valuable feedback.

Thank you for taking the time to review!

Christina Tosch

About the Author

Christina Tosch is a successful chef and renowned cookbook author from Long Grove, Illinois. She majored in Liberal Arts at Trinity International University and decided to pursue her passion of cooking when she applied to the world renowned Le Cordon Bleu culinary school in Paris, France. The school was lucky to recognize the immense talent of this chef and she excelled in her courses, particularly Haute Cuisine. This skill was recognized and rewarded by several highly regarded Chicago restaurants, where she was offered the prestigious position of head chef.

Christina and her family live in a spacious home in the Chicago area and she loves to grow her own vegetables and herbs in the garden she lovingly cultivates on her sprawling estate. Her and her husband have two beautiful children, 3 cats, 2 dogs and a parakeet they call Jasper. When Christina is not hard at work creating beautiful meals for Chicago's elite, she is hard at work writing engaging e-books of which she has sold over 1500.

Make sure to keep an eye out for her latest books that offer helpful tips, clear instructions and witty anecdotes that will bring a smile to your face as you read!

Made in the USA
Middletown, DE
22 May 2022

66076271R00073